VERSE MA

# *Verse Matters*

Edited by Rachel Bower & Helen Mort

VP

First published in 2017 by Valley Press
Woodend, The Crescent, Scarborough, YO11 2PW
www.valleypressuk.com

ISBN 978-1-908853-87-5
Cat. no. VP0104

A CIP record for this book is available
from the British Library.

Cover design by Sail Creative.
Text design by Gerry Cambridge.
Set in Baskerville 10 Pro.

Printed and bound in Great Britain by
TJ International Ltd, Padstow, Cornwall.

# Contents

*Foreword / 9*
*Introduction / 11*

LIZ BERRY
when you came / 13
Kejimakujik / 14
Horse Heart / 15

BASHAR FARAHAT
My Mother's last commandments / 16
Calligraphy by Lama Andoura / 19

RIVER WOLTON
Welcome / 20

SHIRIN TEIFOURI
Nomadic Kitchens / 22

RACHEL BOWER
Sheffield to Aleppo / 23
Amber / 24

SAI MURRAY
Seven Scales / 25

MALIKA BOOKER
Retribution / 27

HELEN MORT
from 'Austerity Circus': Bartek / 28

VICKY MORRIS
Treatment / 30
Ward 2 (Weston Park Hospital) / 32

CHAR MARCH
This is the talking of hands / 33
The 'conservation nightmare' of
the Ballachulish Goddess / 35

MIMI MESFIN (YENENESH)
Missing my Mum / 36

JACOB BLAKESLEY
Nightfall / 38

CAROLE BROMLEY
Writing Desk / 40
Aunt Reed has her say / 41

HANNAH COPLEY
Sorry / 42
Ten Thousand / 43

S J BRADLEY
Weak Heart / 45

NICK ALLEN
Once upon a street in Yorkshire / 49

WENDY PRATT
In the Parole Office / 51

JO IRWIN
Rip Tide / 52

CHARLOTTE ANSELL
Drowning / 54
Emptied / 56

WARDA YASSIN
Victoria Street / 58

LOUISE CLINES
The New Creation (age 4) / 59

CATHERINE AYRES
When I say I think about you every day / 60
Café / 61

ETHEL MAQEDA
Some Friendships are Forever / 62

KATHERINE HENDERSON
How to throw a punch / 69

SEZ THOMASIN
How Donna was Different / 70

BETH DAVIES
Daphne / 73

HOLLIE MCNISH
Fine / 75
Expectations / 76

LAURIE BOLGER
Rubbish / 77

SHELLEY ROCHE-JACQUES
Allgemeinbildung / 78

KATE GARRETT
Gravida 5, Parity 3 / 80

DEBJANEE CHATTERJEE
Still, but not Silent / 81
Indrail Honeymoon / 82

AMY KINSMAN
Untitled / 84

CAROL EADES
A Curious Legacy / 85

SUZANNAH EVANS
The Censored City / 86
How to Live in a City / 87

*Contributor Biographies* / 88
*About the Editors* / 96

# Foreword

As you would expect from Valley Press, one of Yorkshire's leading publishers, these are mainly poems and prose with a northern flavour. The anthology, like Sheffield's famous liquorice allsorts, is a pleasing and diverse mix by 'all sorts' of writers. The contributors are mainly northerners and mainly women; some are writers for whom English is not their first language; some are professional writers, while others are being published for the first time. The editors, both Sheffield-based award-winning writers, have ensured a high standard, and selected these poems and stories for their promise and their power.

DEBJANI CHATTERJEE, MBE
*Sheffield*

## Introduction

We're sitting down to write this on a grey day in February, 2017. Last week a crowd of people watched and filmed a 22-year-old Gambian man drowning in the Venice Grand Canal. Onlookers jeered and shouted racist comments as they watched him die.

Theodor Adorno once famously said that 'to write poetry after Auschwitz is barbaric.' Without suggesting there is a simple meaning to be drawn from Adorno's complex writing, it seems fair to say that we are at a juncture in which it has once again become urgent to ask about the role of art in the face of extreme dehumanisation.

Hundreds of people drown each year fleeing violence in search of a safer life in Europe. One person every four seconds dies of malnutrition. Eight men possess the same wealth as the 3.6 billion people who form the poorest half of the world's population. These are times in which people are increasingly dehumanised and marginalised. Xenophobia, racism and misogyny are rapidly on the rise. How do we continue to live our normal lives in light of all of this? How can we speak about these experiences? How can we turn each injustice into a poetry of resistance, and should we even try?

In his famous 'A Defence of Poetry', Percy Bysshe Shelley said that 'poets are the unacknowledged legislators of the world'. It's been quoted so often that the phrase almost seems clichéd, but Shelley's words still speak to the ability of creative writing to alter our world view in a way that can be empowering. This anthology hopes to confirm the legislative power of fiction, to show that—in times like these—it is more important than ever to celebrate words that attest to being alive—and being human.

This anthology seeks to harness the power of ordinary, extraordinary stories to speak to something true in difficult times and to celebrate everyday, remarkable events. These stories explore moments of sadness, anger, humility and happiness. Through them, we hope to create a space in which less-heard voices can be recognised—a written space for stories that might have been erased by society. We want to insist on human connections in times in which these are being eroded.

Many of the poems included in this book are by writers based in Yorkshire, including some authors for whom English is not their first language. Some of the poems are by refugees, who have sought sanctuary in the UK. Less-known authors are published alongside established writers like Liz Berry, Malika Booker and Hollie McNish. Each piece included in this anthology has a different vista (a kitchen window, a street in Sheffield, a familiar country left behind) and suggests a slightly different way of looking (through the lens of humour, pathos or joy) but what unites them is the effect they had on us as readers: surprising us, making us glad to be alive, making us want to pick up a pen and write.

RACHEL BOWER and HELEN MORT
*February 2017*

LIZ BERRY

*when you came*

i opened my body like a window
in spring    to let you in

with all budded things and silken things
things curled secret upon themselves

i let you in with fat blossom
and april mizzle fine as a web

with the vixen laying down
in the blood pink of dawn

and the robin calling calling
you from the birch

i opened myself
and you made a wum of me

a house ransacked wild
a mansion of red and golden rooms

*wum* / home

## Kejimakujik

There were moments giving birth
when the pain shone
so deeply through my bones
I believed I wanted to walk
into that lake at Kejimakujik,
that silent star-mirroring lake, so deep
it has no trough, no soul;
to slip my skin and slither loose—
an eel, clot dark and sinewy,
my jaw a storm lantern swinging
in the black, my body the sheen
of the lake, of the night
the lake swallowed, an arrow
of black blood quivering
through the water,
my lidless eyes gazing upon
black, my seed pearl teeth singing
of black, of black so black
it shot my heart and spangled my mind
like an electric bolt.

LIZ BERRY

*Horse Heart*

It is a stable in here.
The sodden hay of broken waters,
each of us private and lowing in our stalls
while all night, from the monitors,
the sound of babies' hearts like hooves
stumbling       stamping
through our bodies       up
into the high wet grass of their lives.

How reckless they are—
lost now    then again
in snowy fields of static.
Too fast and they're gone, too slow
and they might never reach us at all
but fall, heads crowned by vetch
and dandelion, noses cold to the belly
of the earth.

Oh these horse nights, these terrible
darkless nights, the endless running
of the herd, fear a hoof
upon my chest.
I lie in my sweats and beckon you up.
Little horse heart, foal,
let my love be your paddock, your bridle,
your trough.

BASHAR FARAHAT

*My Mother's last commandments*
*(originally in Arabic)*

My mother passes by my room every hope
She tracks down my escaping shadows
From my remaining things
A photo, two year old boy, crying
A photo, twenty year old boy, smiling
My first steps, my last school
My best friends, my worst marks
Half souvenirs, in a half memory.
My mother double checks our memory,
The part of it, which survived the last war.
'Your very heart is still here, shrapnel cannot defeat blood
Be careful of forgetfulness, alternative homes and the warmth
      of exiles
Direct your last bag to your first address'
She writes on the wall of absence, erases, cries and then
      writes again,
'Be wherever you want, don't die
Don't care for songs which lead you, stay in the celebrated
                  definite death
Decorated with victory and elegance
Death is death,
And loss is loss, forever
Ignore messengers, books and seduction of war
Fight for a woman, don't fight for a king
Think of a land that shall embrace your far away tomorrow
Think of a land that shall accept you, crowned with sins
Think of a land, fertile for a dream
Be wherever you want
Don't die, don't die, don't die'

*Note:*

p18 shows the original of Bashar Farahat's poem in Arabic.

p19 shows calligraphy created by the artist Lama Andoura as part of the Harbour Project. The line is taken from Bashar's poem, and reads: 'Think of a land, fertile for a dream'.

Lama's artworks are based on calligraphy using the Kufic font. Kufic is the oldest calligraphic form of various Arabic scripts and consists of a modified form of the old Nabataea script. Kufic developed around the end of the 7th century in Kufa, Iraq, from which it takes its name.

Pages 18 and 19 should be turned clockwise for correct viewing.

# آخر وصايا أمي

"بعض قلبك هنا – لا تعلّب القلب الشطآن

لا تكترث بالأغنيات الباعثات على البلاء بخانة الموت الأكيد المحتفي به والمزين بالبطولة والألق

– فاحذر النسيان والوطن النبيل وكل أخوة المنافي

تنفّق الذكرى أو جرّدها الناجي من الحرب الأخيرة ثم تكتب:

أمي تعاتب طيفي الغائي على كتف الغياب

تحمو وتعيد صوغ الشرق في أولى وصاياها الأخيرة ثم تبكي

"دكن حيث شئت ... ولا تمت"

فالموت موت خالٍ
والعهد فقد دائماً
نم جيداً
كل جيداً

فكر بأرض تحتفي هناك البعيد وتخويك مكللاً بالإثم
فكر بأرض تستوي للحلم
"دكن حيث شئت ... ولا تمت"

تحتفي في طفولتي البعيدة/ صورة في عامي الثاني (شقتُ)/ صورة أخرى (شقتُ) / صورة أخرى كل انتظار

أمي تسرّ بغرفتي كل انتظار
أمي تسرّ بغرفتي كل انتظار
ترتّب كل أشيائي على مهل

نصف ذكرى/ نقش ذاكرة بعيدة

"آخر ذكرى الأخيرة دائماً .. نحو البئد"

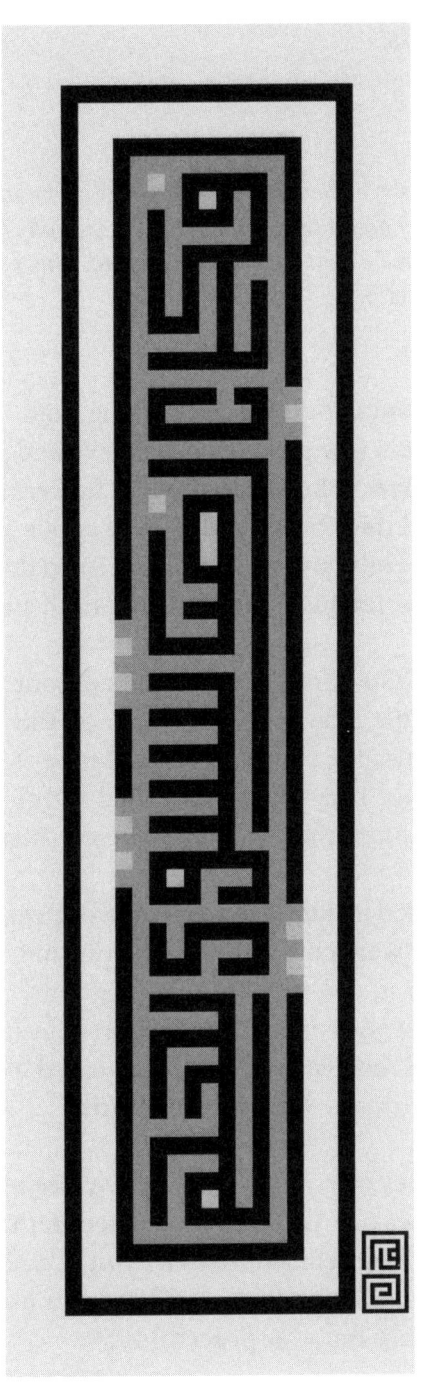

RIVER WOLTON

## Welcome

*The City of Sanctuary movement began in Sheffield in 2005 and sought to build a culture of hospitality and welcome, especially for refugees. The movement has spread across the UK and Ireland. This poem was written for CoS's 10th anniversary.*


Recall the welcomes you've received—the time
you trudged into a town where even bricks and glass
called you 'stranger', shutters slammed, flowers shivered,
stray cats turned their backs and no-one spoke your tongue.
Your pack the weight and awkwardness of coal,
night coming on, the mocking rain, and each step numb.

Doubt growled 'Go home!' but home had gone. Recall
as the light shrank, a door cracked open on the
muttered shadows of a room, a glass of amber tea,
a wary beckoning. They looked as scared as you,
suspicious of your clothes, your stammered thanks;

then you glimpsed a child's face, a game of peek-a-boo
and though you were chilled through, you smiled,
bread was laid out, you sat between the granny
and the youngest with a cracked plate on your lap.
A corner cleared for sleep, your journey eased away
and dawn broke on the bloom of a new day.

Think of the times when those you'd never see again
brought water, wished you well or pointed out the way,
when the earth itself seemed to invite you as a chosen guest
to walk on summer lanes, lean your head against a tree
or float your weary limbs in peaceful bays.

Harvest these memories, for what is refuge
unless freely passed on to others when our brief lives meet.
May we become the welcomes we've received,
and may the call for sanctuary Sheffield's begun
grow loud, till every street rings out with
'Welcome. Welcome. Welcome.'

SHIRIN TEIFOURI

## *Nomadic Kitchens*

Some kitchens are wanderers
they are born late-comers
to busy dining tables
they can be spotted by their naked windows
and jumbled collection of cups and plates
picked up on the way
they never talk about their lost cutleries
they pass rocky mountains
that's why they carefully wrap the memories
of grandma's china set,
they are not eloquent
that's why they fail to explain how exotic recipes
can easily heat their oven's chest
they are surrogate mothers of lonely diners
on Christmas day
nomadic kitchens are shy and restless
they are scared to be intimate
if somewhere faraway
between mountains and deserts
they could finally undress a tangerine
and lure a guest...
you only know them gone
when sun-dried fruit of a womb
is miscarried in the cellar of the happy house.

*Sheffield to Aleppo*

*It's only a firework,* I whisper
thumb tucked into her palm
but her eyes reflect a spark
that tells me that somewhere

she knows this isn't quite true—
that a shot can echo when stars skim seas
that shrapnel can whistle through waves
screeching fear in bruising skies

and I stroke floss hair and sweet bun cheeks
damp from steam, breathing milk
and I ache for it *only to be fireworks*

for thumbs in the dark to be enough
to stop glazed buns cracking in the dust
for shells that spill only golden fish
for grazes that heal with the fizz

of a rocket and I kneel
in the night and feel her sleep.

RACHEL BOWER

*Amber*

You sat on the sofa and watched tears leak
as I told you *I am a milk machine—*
*I can only offer this, everyone says*
*put him down, he cannot be hungry, my blood*
*turns the milk pink, I can offer nothing else.*

*You said milk is what he needs, you are all*
*he needs, you are growing a person*
*take him into your bed and do what you feel.*

I am all he needs. I hauled myself taller then,
mouth remembering my great great
grandma, before shame, before clockwork babies
when sisters knew milk has raspberry threads
and aunties pressed cabbage on breasts

and even though you never came back
you left resin on the cushion and my milk shone gold
and we sat for weeks in your glow.

*Seven Scales*

*One, two, three, four, five,*
*once we caught our fish alive.*
*Six, seven...*

Seven.
Sacred number. Lucky. Deadly sins.
Nguzo Saba (seven principles):
Afrikan family values or
spoiler alert:
Brad Pitt and a severed head
in the film of the same name.

This severing of heads,
severing of thought, of language.
Severing, silencing, sectioning:
a constant throughout our culture.
Not unique to recent barbarisms.

Quote:
Colonial impressions of the continent
report shock at how lenient punishments were.
Jail cells virtually unknown, capital punishment rare,
policed by community, elders wisdom.

*Seven, eight, nine, ten—*
*We let them go. Again.*

The hands we fed bit us.
Took our fish.
Processed our waters,
Coated us in breadcrumbs
Sold us our own fingers.

On the one hand, we have a fish
On the other finger...
Do we bite the hand that feeds lies to us?
The other hand behind the back
with a bludgeon mallet. mullet.

Give the women, men the means to realise
that this fish
was stolen from them in the first place
Our plaice. Our halibut. Our collective habitat.
Their Haliburton
And we shall eat for more than a day.

## *Retribution*

And on that day we banked our canoes
on hopeless shore. Our anorexic timber too
frail to float, rotted and we sunk.

And on that day bells were silenced,
their severed tongues floated like leaves
into freshly dug graves in the ground.

The earth pommelled those rainy tongues
into carcass flavoured milk. Grass tattooed
our left foot, etching acid onto our ankle bone.

Our right foot had swum in reeking water
where dead fish floated belly up,
guts emptying to oil our passive toes.

We howled for lemons to suck bitter rind
but yellow had been deported from our
sepia land, with no leave to revoke,

so we nestled our babies, for the faint hum
of faith, then placed them into chubby palms
that pulverised their skin with thorns.

*From* 'Austerity Circus'

*Bartek*

the wire pulls taut
the wire is a single thought
the wire is a line in pencil
through my name on the ringmaster's list

neat flick-of-the-wrist      I close
my eyes      rub it out      my body
goes before me like a shout in a dark cave

down there      counted rows of seats
overhead      a tapered roof
the colour of boiled sweets

music muted as I balance
sway      my arms above my head
the fat announcer      miles away

*Will Bartek reach the other side*
*and win the right to stay? Folks,*
*you decide!*

some of them lob      oranges
some chuck bricks      all of them
miss      sing songs      throw curses
in their single tongue

the wire is a note
the wire is an open throat
I drew the wire in the sand at Sopot as a child
until the sea went wild and wanted the beach back

slow clap      I'm halfway
wobbling in the centre of the ring
a sawdust stink      glass breaks
behind the bar

*Guys, no-one else has got this far!*
*Can Bartek make it*
*and become a citizen?*

lights swim      my blank face
steady steps     slow
pace    the circus in me
like a seam      I'm stitched to air

the wire is a word no-one said
the wire is a hole in the head
the wire is a line of piss trickling down my leg

one side      sunlight
one side      strangers willing me
to fall

the questions  cameras
afterwards      I say
I've done this
my whole life
that's all

## Treatment

At times, he'll bring out the comedy from it all,
like how he waited hospital hours and succumbed to the soup
that was more like the sauce that comes with baked beans.

He'll tell you things like this, while you wince
as his fingertips become nerve-heavy thumb prints,
rubbing moisture into the red-raw winter of your skin.

Once a week, you'll take a seat while he stands
to pick through your matted curls with a hair grip, to see what
he can salvage, his shoulders sore from stooping.

And every third week, he'll rub your feet to distract you
from the pain of the ice cap's -22, and they'll pump you
as you watch, with pesticides, clear and red.

On Tuesdays, tired, he'll wear gloves that never fit,
to clean the line that connects arm to heart, and secure the bung
like a rolled-up cigarette, while all the time you bark instructions.

Like in those first weeks, months before, when he'll lift you
in and out of bed (the way the nurse says is best) and he won't sit
in peace and rest, until you are sleeping.

He'll be your left arm, and the movement of a broom you'll use
to knit back nerves, circling shoulder to elbow in a curve on the
        floor
his eyes willing you a little more every time.

He'll remove your paper knickers, your chest padded
and bandaged, and you'll shower, for the first time, balanced,
between IV stand and him.

And days before, when the surgeon walks in, he'll come alive
working through questions you typed, making notes
as he goes, because he knows you'll forget everything else said,

after they tell you, one week before you go under, that the MRI
measured 5, not the ultrasound 2.4, and they will have to
take it all. The lymph nodes in your arm. The chance of more.

That's when he will be holding you,
like when he'll tell you
he will still think you're beautiful.

And you will feel it.
You will feel it.

VICKY MORRIS

## Ward 2 (Weston Park Hospital)

We are taking up beds,
bodies with the same lead weights
on shoulders we have become unsure of.
The four of us, ladies in Ward 2 waiting,
with our drips and PICCs, and cannulated veins,
wondering when we can go home again.

Maureen forgets to take her tablets.
The nurses scold with laughter.
She offers back giggles from 70 years earlier.
Ashrita cries over a text from her ex.
She had a tooth pulled yesterday.
They give her morphine for the pain.

Denise is the most cheerful.
She is waiting for the okay on a final trial,
asks us all to order bacon for her
when breakfast comes around.
*You wouldn't get this at the Northern General,*
she jokes, chomping it down.

Her husband, Brian, is the *Daily Mail* newshound.
He soapboxes the corner well past visiting hours,
says he's voting UKIP on Thursday,
says the money should be spent on cancer drugs.
He wants anything
that could save his wife.

## *This is the talking of hands*

My talk. Not yours.
Your hands are clumsy, inaccurate,
fumble things round the twisted way.
Your eyes tell me they hold my pain,
but you know nothing of pain,
or the holding of it, or the way
pain held me in joy. You know nothing
of joy. You want to know only of pain,
as if this is the significant thing.

My daughter is eight years old, and makes
the stage look very big. I strapped her feet
into the gold sandals. She is dipping
and bobbing, her back a swan's neck,
her fingers arch back in perfect half-moons.
She smiles. Her tiny pearl teeth gleam. She smiles.
She quivers the long golden nails that I have tied
with wire into her fingertips.

These are the exercises to get the hands to bend.
This is the stinging oil that is massaged in hot,
this is the leather-lined vice, this is the repetition,
this is the repetition, this is the repetition.
It must all begin at suckling age.
The exercises, the oil, the vice.

This is the talking of hands. My voice
is clear and sharp. High as a loon parrot's call.
Yours, the muffled crashing of a rhino
in forest far off. Your fingers are long, slender;
knuckles that allow your ring to slide too easy.
We have all seen how your eyes slide on our sons.

Yes, your hands will win *Most Lovely* contest,
but they mumble, mutter, stutter, stumble.
They can never catch the quickness of my speech,
the deftness of my laughter at you. They are never
going to wring the neck of a junglefowl, they speak
with sliding marks on paper, they are hands
to smother life from something,
not give it a clean end.

## The 'conservation nightmare' of the Ballachulish Goddess

Wit the fuck huv they dun tae ma heid?
I look like yon Norwegian wifie wailin oan a pier!
I yaist tae be bonny, wi' a bit ay flesh oan ma bains.
Aye well, wud then—a bit ay wud oan ma wud.

See yon label—bletherin' oan aboot me hoddin'
some 'phallic symbol' in ma hon?
Wit a load ay baws! Cun they no' see
it's a spurtle fur ma parritch?

If I'd been some big bugger Odin, or that
auld bastard Thor (he hud a mooth oan him that wan)
they'd huv ta'en guid care o' me fur sure!
Wudnae huv let *thair* tadgers dry oot!

Aw ma bits ur yeukie an' raw—ah'v been needin'
a guid claw, a guid drouk, a guid shaggin'
fur centuries! Yous look a poustie laddie, ken.
Aye yoo! Dinnae look awa'—I've got ma wee

quartz e'en fixit oan yur braw bahookie
and ma big scrabbilit fingurs'll be gi'in yoo
an affi guid feel—soon as I bluiter oot this gless.
Whoar ur yous awa' tae?! Ahm wantin' ma hochmagandie!

## Missing My Mum
*(originally in Amharic)*

*—Yenafikot engurguro: the song that people hum when they are*
*missing someone*

In the garden of my memories, the birds are calling
but I only hear the echo of my mother's voice.
She sits in the shade of the apple tree
her soft voice crosses the mountains and the seas.

She sits alone, humming the song of loneliness.
All day she sits at home, her children far away.
I miss her too. I don't want to lose her.

Live a long life Mum, and one day, God willing,
I will see you again.

# እናቴ ናፈቅሽኝ

ለዓይን ከሚማርክ ከአትክልቱ ስፍራ
ለጆሮ ጣዕም ካለው የወፎቹ ዜማ
ጋራ ሸንተረሩን ባህሩን አቋርጦ

    ይሰማኛል ዜማሽ
    የናፍቆት እንጉርጉሮ
    ያ ለሆሳስ ድምፅሽ
    በምናቤ አሰብኩሽ
    ከዛሩ ጥላ ስር
    ብቸኝነት ከቦሽ
    ናፍቆት አስጨንቆሽ

እናቴ ናፈቅሽኝ
አልጣሽ ኑሪልኝ
ላይሽ እመጣለሁ
ጌታ ቢፈቅድልኝ

*This is the Amharic original of the poem*
*by Mimi Mesfin (Yenenesh) opposite.*

JACOB BLAKESLEY

## *Nightfall*

### 1

A pool of water dusked with silt,
little creatures flutter and flake apart,
they glide, crumbling, over the musical surface,
veined with smoky water.

Time weaves me with sheets of rain.

### 2

Night falls bit by bit.
Strewn with embers, I fall with her.

I have not yet learned the art of plummeting.
My song's measure is in abeyance.

### 3

*les espaces infinis...*

A cipher ringed by two
endless black strands.

Grained pomegranates scatter
bitter seeds.

The light's repose
hardly lingers.

4

Ruins.

The grass—
warriors' lost dreams—
throttles skeletons.

Rain slices apart
apple-scented breezes.

5

In the beginning is my end.

CAROLE BROMLEY

*Writing Desk*

I found it in a junk shop in Bishy Road;
the label said *Lady's Writing Desk.*

So pretty with its red leather top,
its slim, turned legs, drawer with brass catch.

A man would need to spread himself,
his important work laid out around him

while I perch on a cushioned lady's chair
writing poems with a lady's fountain pen.

But it's worm-eaten, my desk, rough to the touch,
I run my fingers over fragile tunnels,

find little piles of fine sand in the drawer
on my pencils, my ruler, my hole punch

where creatures have burrowed out and flown
to attack the stairs, the floors, the rafters.

CAROLE BROMLEY

*Aunt Reed has her say*

Well, of course I locked her in the red room.
You'd have done the same. So sly,
sneaking around, hiding behind curtains.

He should never have said yes.
Typical of his sister to go and die on us
and just like him to send for the baby.

I hated the sickly, whining, pining thing.
I'd have soon have been charged
with a pauper brat out of a workhouse.

And why me? I'd enough of my own.
Eliza and Georgiana to marry off
and John such a handful.

Mostly I left Jane to the servants,
couldn't stand the sight of her.
That book was the last straw.

How was I to know there'd be typhoid?
At least she got her comeuppance
with that sign round her neck.

And I wasn't about to lend a hand
in lifting her to prosperity,
not after the things she said.

Cruel? Give me strength. I was *kind*.
She'd have starved without me,
she'd have ended up on the streets.

Some people don't know they're born.

*Sorry*

*for H*

Tucked in the gap between sorrow
and soul you catch something of their weight,

hold yourself heavy as you push past
the pregnant woman carrying the carton of eggs,

and hang back under your shelter of *rrs*
as the young man ignores you in the queue to get on.

Somewhere near home, though, you lighten.
The number 84 pulls out and the road stretches

past the valley of your consonants and you glimpse,
over the horizon, first your reflection, and then

your proximity to song. You're close enough now
to reach and touch your leg to his through the seats.

Stretching out, you exhale that single O
that dances on the tip of your tongue.

## Ten Thousand

All the ways a person can be made
to understand the darkness in their heart—

to know they've been lost—
can be traced back to coal.

Coal, through and through.
Coal. It's a better rule to live by,

singing as it does of *the earth's inside,*
of stain and cinder, of burning

red like the raw edges of a wound.
Coal. It's what grief becomes

if pressed upon, moment
after moment added to the pile.

Some hurts aren't meant to disappear
but to blacken,

to roll in on themselves and stoke up,
ready for the blaze.

Like that cough you've had
since the day your daughter died.

That is coal. That is the inside too.
The black bile peats, hardens,

ready to hock itself up
in a cloud of smoke and soot.

This time ten thousand days
is long enough to line your lungs.

Now you sit, heavy and black,
and wait to make diamonds.

## Weak Heart

When I was a little girl I had a weak heart. A doctor discovered a murmur back when I was a fat legged baby. I hardly noticed, in those days, that mother and I were alone. She said he told her to keep me from strain—any type. Things I was not allowed to do included: running, sledging, cycling, going on rollercoasters, swimming, or skating (ice or roller). Aged six I led the life of a Benedictine monk.

Aged seven I became very interested in animals. Barnyard things, like pigs and cows. I thought I might become a country vet, and begged my mother to take me to the urban farm. She said: 'I'm sorry, my pet. I just think it's too dangerous.' She was frightened that an animal might jump out of its house and give me a shock.

Instead, we went to the library. Three times a week after school and first thing in the morning Saturdays. There were no dangers there. I used to read under a map of the world, books piled up around me like hard backed tower blocks.

Much of the library stock was donated by the hospital. They had a lot of books on Biology and Anatomy, all full of pictures and diagrams. A boy drawn with his chest open, revealing the heart inside. Closer, a picture of the heart itself, all four chambers. Red raw and bloody, like fat slabs of meat.

*A blood clot can occur in any otherwise healthy body,* read one section. That part had photos. Blood clots were black, all of them. The largest had been laid on a white top and placed next to a fifty pence piece to illustrate its size.

It was a good job my mother did not know I read these books. The pictures would have horrified her. *Infection! Cholesterol! Tumours!* They were better than any horror movie, and best of all, completely factual. Malignant tumours getting fat on healthy cells. Immune disorders that make white blood cells attack one another. It is not the world that is full of terror, I discovered, but one's own body. *If the weak heart doesn't kill you,* I started to say to myself, *any one of these dozen of other completely unexpected disorders could!*

And then one Saturday my mother said, 'No library today.'

Breath caught in my throat. I had been looking forward to reading the final part of *Secondary Conditions of the Pulmonary System.* Had she discovered, I wondered, what horror stories I read every day? 'Why not?' I asked.

Crouching down, she said: 'I've made a very special friend, darling. A friend called Terry. He's coming to visit today, and I want you to be good.' Good! I was always good. 'You'll like him,' she said.

I did not like him. Special Uncle Terry was broad, with a half-bald ginger thatch, and had two boys who didn't live with him. When he arrived he put a pound coin in my palm and said, 'You can occupy yourself for the afternoon, can't you?'

I said, 'I'll read.' I went upstairs, and he and my mother went to her room.

I was cross about missing out on going to the library. I'd finished reading all of the books I'd checked out, and so I sat with my soft toys about me, playing that each was a real animal, near birth or seriously cancerous, and each in need of my help. 'Emergency biopsy!' I shouted at a glass-eyed bear. 'You're too young for the glue factory!' On the adjoining wall, I could hear the sound of furniture moving.

It was too bad that Uncle Terry kept coming to visit. My mother coloured her hair dark, because he liked it that way, and started wearing a pair of gold hoop earrings which he'd bought for her. He brought me an old watch with a cracked strap, and said it was for measuring my heartbeat.

Yet he didn't come every night. Mother said he was 're-searching business opportunities' on the nights he wasn't with us. She used to get skittish. Reading under the duvet I'd hear her pick up the phone, dial, and listen, and silently replace the receiver. I counted eight, nine, ten times a night, some nights.

She was so preoccupied, she hardly noticed what I was doing. The freedom was marvellous. I ran. I jumped. I climbed trees. Nobody told me to be careful.

It was on one of these play-outs that I saw Uncle Terry. I was in the park, high up the weeping willow, when he walked by with two apple cheeked boys who looked very like him, and a woman in impractical high heels. All of them were laughing.

They followed the path around the duck pond, and I caterpillared along the branch to try and keep them in sight. But not having had the practise at holding on, I fell. My friends later said they could almost see stars circling my head as I landed.

My mother was there, in the hospital, when I woke. Clutching my hand, she wailed: 'I should have been taking proper care of you.' Her hair was turning mousey where she'd let the roots grow out.

The ward was full of little girls with serious conditions. Over the floor from me was a girl hooked to a drip, her skin paler than ice. 'Where's Uncle Terry?' I asked.

'He isn't coming,' she said. 'I couldn't get hold of him.' Her voice sounded hollow, like a drainpipe.

The doctor came, with his long fingers and his cold stethoscope. 'Tough little thing, aren't you?' he said. He listened to my heart. 'That's a good heartbeat,' he said. 'It nearly made me go deaf in one ear.'

'But her heart ...' began my mother.

'Yes, her heart,' he said. 'A little irregular. But I wouldn't worry about that.' He stood up, and his lab coat fell straight around his knees. 'I shouldn't think it would bother her too much.' He patted my hand smartly, and walked away.

She stared after him. Her eyes were like overflowing sinks. 'This would never have happened if I'd been watching you,' she said.

My cast was white, fresh, ready to be written on. I wriggled my toes, knowing that if I was a horse, they would have shot me. No farmer wants a shire with a weak leg. 'Don't worry, mum,' I said. 'It'll be fine. It'll heal just as strong as before.'

'Don't worry about that,' she said, and her hand closed over mine, with the strength of a blood pressure monitor. 'I'm never taking my eyes off you again.'

## Once Upon a Street in Yorkshire

*In Memory of Jo Cox, MP for Batley and Spen Valley,*
*died 16th June 2016.*

there was a pub   there was a bookmakers
a post office and a library   a Co-op   and a butchers
there was a grocers and there was a bakers

the bus-stop on either side marked the start
or the end of the line     there were children
making their way to school     and there was a murder

there were cars parked intermittently
sometimes a van   or a truck unloading   double-parked
young men on motorbikes louder than sense

flowers wrapped in plastic   tied to a lamp-post
and a smudged card   all condolence lost to wind and the rain
down the gutter   down the drain     and there was a murder

there were young mothers   side by side with pensioners
there were straight and gay and many who didnt care anyway
a christian went into the butchers while a hindu

went into the library   a jew helped an old muslim woman
carrying her shopping in recycled bags that advertised
the local donkey sanctuary     and there was a murder

some atheists gathered   one said he was agnostic
but no one believed him   a teenage girl chewed gum
and flicked at her phone as she waited for friends

and there was a murder
a car blew its horn
and there was a murder

## *In the Parole Office*

The lads are leaf litter
blown in through
the gaps they fell through.
Cheeky laddish types,
thuggish hard man types
all of them little lads
in the orange plastic seats.
There are buckets of boys
here skittles of boys and one
girl thrown like a hand grenade
into the middle of them. Tick
tick says the girl brokenly
to the broken boys who rub
themselves against her oily
camouflage. tick tick.

JO IRWIN

*Rip Tide*

Home was in the air, seat F4,
A giant's view, taffeta sea
And a tumultuous cloud rug
Through fogged panes I searched

In the sponge of the rain forest
Scarlet flame, Bird of Paradise,
Swooning with salt, sweet tang of sweat,
Sarong petals unfurled to bask

In the cool fan of a reed hut
On a sagging mattress on the
Edge of a mesh room, mosquitoes
Flicking sanguine proboscises

On a beach on a sand pillow
Me and the others scanned star-pinned
Skies, spinning stories of past lives
Unpacked from burgeoning backpacks

Stuffed in with crumpled shorts, shirts, holed
Off coloured pants, knives, lamps, brush, paste
The stone mother, the lost brother
The girl left by her lover

Foam erased our footprints, waves shussed us

Faster I spread over land, liquid
Absorbing towns, cities, stalkers,
Hawkers, no dam to capture me

In the sea
The angels of surf glistening
In the stark sun, crested waves licked
And gulped me up
Just like that
Rolled in sea jaws, I tumbled
Ripped and gummed by tides
Head over heels in love with the land
A rolling grain fishing for breaths

I thought they would find me face down
Far from my spread towel
I panged
And the sea left me

Lolled on a curled wave onto dry, hard sand
I scuttled
Onto the empty page of sand

CHARLOTTE ANSELL

*Drowning*

When the news breaks and the tide cannot be turned
I find comfort in the Muslim call to prayer on TV,
its mathematical calm laps over me
like today as I paint, the ripples of chatter
from the Eastern European family fishing
on the opposite bank of the canal,
I sink into the lull of incomprehensible words

but the laughter of children is the same,
the cheers when they catch a fish.
I wouldn't eat anything from this water
maybe they wouldn't either,
I push my assumptions down, drown them in paint.

We co-exist in this subdued day
Cloud muffling out any extremes,
the odd phrase in English reaches me
and when they leave, a man calls out
*'beautiful painting—you come paint my house?*
*See you next time!'*

Not everything can be covered, made new.
When my friend's appeal for asylum was refused
I went round; the nakedness of the packing boxes
the panic in her daughters' eyes
and her without her hijab.
Somehow I couldn't hug her
seeing her so exposed.
After three long years they let her stay.

Isn't that all anyone wants,
a safe place to call home?
I go back to painting,
the grey green expanse grows,
soothing my eyes.

If only
it didn't remind me of the cold sea,
the slip slop of the brush like the slap of waves,
lifting a dress to expose a nappy
breaking over pliable limbs,
a swirl of dark curls,
such a little face,
as if in repose.

*Emptied*

I didn't feel you slip away,
cocooned I waited
for proof on a screen.

You were there alright,
my nearly child
but the probe

was as silent as snow,
no heartbeat thrum
of horse's hooves,

leaving me to face
alone the vicissitudes
of the nurse who

shouted at me
for my emerald toes
that apparently I should

have scraped clean
before the surgeon in the
ice white box of theatre,

scraped me clean of you.
I left numb, vacuumed;
nothing to show or keep,

no fuzzy blizzard shot
of obscured head and tiny feet,
no blood stained sheets,

no memento
to stave off the aftermath,
and your dad's sister

with her usual tact,
saying a fortune teller told her
you would have been a boy.

*Victoria Street*

If buildings had feelings, Victoria Street
would need a therapist.

Thugs, imams, families, woman beaters,
and a pub, reside in anarchy,

rubble, stray cats and love.
No *Morning* to each other.

The postman knows to knock once.
Children are ushered from pavements

after Maghrib. Billowing garnets brush past
sloganed crop tops. The breeze

brings the Adaan, Dubstep and sirens,
the smell of the sauna, the smoke of incense.

Out front, my father breaks his fast,
chews dates, offers a cautious smile

to those with heavy eyes across the way.
These parallel buildings demonstrate

difference, but reflect something
of the same. The street is anything

but royal,
we share a common fate.

## *The New Creation (age 4)*

*A found poem*

Is it the end of the world yet?
What is the end of the world about?
Is it the end of the world in Sheffield?
The end of the world isn't a time of peace, is it?

You never die in the new creation.
There's no scary dreams in the new creation.
No boa constrictors eat you there.
You can't get a train to the new creation.
You'd run out of diesel.
Why can't Nanna Mary get a train back
to normal living?
You can send a letter to the new creation.
It's like the whole world is in the new creation.
It's very far away from here.
I think it's in Dublin. Or maybe Manchester.

CATHERINE AYRES

*When I say I think about you every day*

I mean your heart's small particulars,
its stitches, I'm pressing them to mine,
I mean your eyelashes, I'm kissing them
with blinks, I mean our backs are blessed
at our kitchen sinks when we slump in a slant
of light we can't see, I mean our fingertips
leave moons on the glass, I mean the white horse,
the liquid deer, I mean sometimes I fold into an owl
and scalp our furred hearts clean, I mean look up,
you're luminous.

*Café*

One day you will deliberately sit
at the table in the sun—with your tea,
your open book, a napkin, a fruit scone—
and turn your thirsty face into the light,
a small act, but a necessary one,
because the ghosts that swirl inside your skin,
(the ones who stretch black moons under your eyes),
will shrivel in the window's gentle flare
and for a moment all of them will rise
like lost balloons and drift off out of sight.
You'll sit, then, with your tea, your book, your scone,
your face all warm, the morning in your hair;
the sun will fade, a seagull will float by,
a single pearl across an oyster sky.

## Some Friendships are Forever

The first time I saw them I thought they were floating. They were perched on a revolving glass pedestal in the window of Meikles Department Store on Main Street. I don't know how long I stood there with my face pressed against the panes watching the pedestal go round and round like a very slow whirlwind that compels one to watch rather than run for cover. The glare of the midmorning sun flooding the displays in the window, created a shimmering mirage that made the shoes look like they were encircled by translucent silk.

But that was thirty years ago. Thirty years, in which a war had been fought and won and some battles had been surrendered. They were thirty years in which I had also bought and worn many pairs of shoes, styles and colours. I could do that. This wasn't Rhodesia anymore. A job at The Harare Institute of Technology meant I never had to wear uncomfortable shoes or cast-offs again. The last time I did was when I interviewed for my first job after Secondary School. I took the shoes off halfway through the interview. They were too small two sizes too small and my feet were on fire. I didn't get the job.

It didn't make sense that a similar pair of deep, wine-red, peep-toe high heeled shoes, that I thought had lost me a friend all those years ago and haunted me all my life, lay nestled on a bed of crumpled copy of *Mail and Guardian* of the 15th of January 2000, in a box on top of my desk. They lay side by side, facing opposite directions, heel to toe. I poked one then the other with a trembling finger, the way we used to poke snakes when the boys had killed them in the school playground. I poked and prodded until they stood upright. They were size seven and nearly new, the 'Made in Italy' sign still visible on the inside.

Hands still trembling, I sat down.

The second hand on the wall clock sounded as though it was right inside my head. My eyes started to sting. I was either sweating or crying.

I had prayed for a sign for a long time until I remembered that God does things in his own time and that ancestors don't do signs of the nature I sought. All I needed to know was that my obsession with the shoes had not destroyed Rura's life and that she had turned out alright. These shoes had arrived too late.

I eased the newspaper out, taking care not to touch them. They had been sent from somewhere in South Africa within the month.

*

The package had arrived early one morning. The postman was a bald, burly man who never got off his bicycle to deliver the mail properly. He tossed everything, regardless of shape, size or weight. Telegrams bearing sad news; letters from loved ones in far off places, dreaded school reports; food parcels from relatives in parts of the country where the harvests were better; bills and all sorts of packages, even the ones with the 'fragile' label all came hurtling towards the recipients so that they didn't have enough time to steel themselves for the impact. I let the small, rectangular piece of paper float and land softly on the concrete veranda floor before retrieving it.

It was a receipt for a parcel. There was no indication of what the parcel might be or who it was from.

*

There is such a thing as wanting something so much that the thing starts to want you more, someone had once told me. Miss Watson had told us the story of a girl called Karen and the red shoes that had so stuck to her feet that the executioner had to chop them off to set her free. It made me shudder to remember.

Perhaps this was my punishment for forgetting about all the places good quality, comfortable shoes were supposed to take me, forgetting about all the selfless things I was going do for the 'less privileged' once I had marched all the way to the top. Mine had become a selfish, comfortable life surrounded by pairs and pairs of shoes that had destroyed my desire to march anywhere or for anything.

No one else knew about the shoes and Rura was dead, had been dead for over ten years. My mother had called me with the news one evening to tell me: 'They have found your friend.'

'Mmm,' I said.

'She's coming home.'

'Mmm,' I said again. I knew how to play her game.

'She's coming home, feet first,' I knew she wanted me to ask what she meant but I didn't.

I can't remember why I missed the funeral.

*

It all started one hot October morning when I couldn't bear the monotony of school anymore. As I walked to school that morning the fields were still wet with dew but clouds of steam rose from the earth and I could tell that the morning assembly was going to be hell. The sun seemed to drop nearer with every step.

I thought if I had to sing 'London's burning' and 'pour on water' one more time it would either kill me or I would say something that would land me in serious trouble. I had been thinking about it for a long time and had come to the conclusion that the people of London should 'pour on water' themselves instead of expecting us to run down to Jeka river, then all the way to London and back again, all in time for mental maths at half past eight, in the sweltering heat and the baking sand. If you had to sing 'London's Burning' in perpetual canons in the scorching heat, with your bare feet slowly getting roasted you would also imagine you were actually putting out the great fire. So, instead of saying to Miss Watson, 'Miss Watson, the sun is very hot where we stand in lines singing 'London's burning' until we flood London with our sweat. We don't want to get involved and we shouldn't have to put out a fire in London…,' and getting myself in the grandmother of all troubles, with Mr Bergeron the headmaster, I decided to skip school to go and look in shop windows in the town centre.

I got to the school gate and waited for Rura. I didn't want to do it alone and Rura, I knew, would do it with me. She didn't play with the other children much. She was different, 'special' Miss Watson said. She had large brown eyes that had no sparkle in them. I thought it might make her happy to see beautiful things in town. I wished to see what her eyes looked like when they sparkled.

It was my cousin Maria's fault. She continually beguiled us with descriptions of all the glamorous things we could look at in shop windows in the town centre. Maria said a lot of things. There were faraway places where the sun never set and the shops stayed open all day and all night she'd tell us. We listened with our mouths wide open.

Maria wore shoes and a uniform to school so she knew about a lot of things, everyone agreed. She said if you hadn't seen the things they had in the shops in town then you hadn't seen anything yet. 'It's like you have been blind all your life', she said. Besides, in the township the shops kept everything behind the counter and you had to point to what you wanted to buy. The shop assistant would then get the item from the shelf or from a box under the counter. I didn't even go into town to buy clothes. All mine, my sisters' and my brothers' clothes and shoes were made by various people in the township. So at ten years old, I had never been to the town centre.

Maria claimed she had once passed through Main Street in a rich relative's car. 'I swear to you, there were lights and things and people sitting around tables in the shops and out-side, eating and drinking.' I tried hard to imagine it but I didn't know what white people ate.

We were only going to look at shops on Main Street. I want-ed to look at books and cakes and sweets. There was so much to see but we were going to be quick, I assured Rura. 'We will be back before school is finished.'

We walked for a long time but only got to town after mid-day. I now know that we walked seven kilometres to town and seven kilometres back home. Rura was also an anxious child and her parents were well-known for the roaring rows they had and the attendant injuries that extended to the chil-dren and the dogs. 'We should go home', she pleaded.

'One more shop, Greatermans... It's the biggest shop in the world. It's a department store, with everything', I coaxed. I knew we were going to be in trouble anyway so I figured I should make the best of it.

And then we saw the shoes!

Although Rura was getting increasingly worried she couldn't move either. In some collective dazzlement we stopped and stared with our mouths wide open.

There were other spectacular things on display in the win-dow. Mannequins, all nine of them a shiny jet black, wear-ing wedding dresses so white it hurt the eyes to look; hats and wigs that made me think of the masquerade dancers that sometimes paraded through the dusty streets of the town-ship and various electrical machines that I had never seen before. I knew they were electrical. I knew this because one of my friends had a distant cousin who worked as a house-maid in the suburbs. She said her cousin had told her that her madam in the suburbs had a lot of machines and that she even had one that washed the clothes while she sat and drunk a glass of *Mazoe*. I wasn't sure about the *Mazoe* but I believed her about the machines. I asked my father because he worked in a factory.

'He he he', he laughed. 'They are clever these white people. They have machines for everything. One of these days they will create one that makes babies for them while they play lawn bowling in Harare Gardens. He he he.'

He was a vulgar man, my father.

I should have been paying more attention to the machines. I remembered that one time when some boys skipped school to go and look at trains and were allowed to tell everyone about it at assembly. They didn't get into trouble. Perhaps there was a machine in this window that nobody else at school had heard about. That would earn me more than a week of envious looks and the coveted status of being a member of that distinguished class of people who were worth having their names dropped into conversations. There would be people from my school who I didn't even know existed who would be saying to their admiring friends, neighbours and acquaintances, 'My friend Tina, from school, has been to town...' or 'A girl from the school next to ours...' This would happen until someone's uncle decided to go overseas and the whole family went to the airport and saw aeroplanes. The machines would then become as insignificant and as insipid as owning a radio had become after Coca Cola ran the 'win a radio' campaign and people drank so much coca cola the whole township was awash with little red round radios. I would then have to join the insignificant band of name droppers but I would have had my time in the limelight and saved us a whipping.

I considered all this in the first few seconds of staring at the shoes and was quite aware that when I got into trouble for skipping school to go into town and said I had looked at a pair of shoes, it would sound lame. It did not matter that these shoes were not like the ordinary black plastic shoes that our fathers wore to work or the black pumps 'MaTomi' that we wore to church on Sundays and to school when there was an important visitor.

For an instant, a split second, I started to get an uneasiness creeping from within the belly. I remembered my grandmother telling me about a snake so beautiful it catches prey by hypnotising it. The beautiful patterns on its back create such a dazzling display as it slowly glides and spirals towards its prey that the prey remains rooted to the spot, mesmerised into immobility. Later, I discovered that that story was my grandmother's attempt at talking to me about boys.

I convinced myself that there was a lot to be learnt from the shoes or they wouldn't be sharing the window with the machines and the wedding dresses. They looked like the kind of shoes one wore to march away from poverty and hunger. I imagined myself wearing these shoes and walking out of the township towards a better life somewhere, I didn't know where but I knew better life wasn't in the township or in our country. An older boy from school who had later left to join the freedom fighters once told us about Rosa Parks and we listened with our mouths wide open. I imagined Rosa Parks had worn shoes like these when she walked onto that Cleveland Avenue bus on that fateful Thursday evening. You don't fight and win battles barefoot or in ill-fitting shoes. No one would take you seriously. That's how I knew Rosa Parks was wearing shoes like these when she got on that Cleveland bus.

*

Of course we were in the grandmother of all troubles when we got home although we didn't mention the shoes. That was the last time I spoke to Rura. She didn't come to school after that. The last time I saw her she was carrying some clothes in a plastic bag and catching a bus to somewhere, I don't know where.

Then my mother called to say they had found her and she was coming home, feet first.

KATHERINE HENDERSON

*How to throw a punch*

a human haunch
caught clockwise last night
hit
hit
hit
the bit that will bruise           tomorrow
hurt it til it hurts it             in the morning
                                    then

make back seams in bones
that need a night of darning
knit fists of flesh back together
knuckle muscles

shift beneath mantle
tectonic plates trade places
rise up,
blue,
volcanic

SEZ THOMASIN

*How Donna Was Different*

Donna was different.

When the girls in the class would slice
The air with sidelong eyes,
Furtively compare
Their work with each others'
And affect despair
'Oh look at yours
It's so GOOD
Mine's rubbish
I'm such an idiot!'
Quietly confident of cries of
'No, that's GOOD!
Don't talk rubbish
It's better than mine, that
It's BRILLIANT!'
We all tried to do it
The false modesty contest
Except Donna
She wasn't bothered
She cut right through it with
'Yours are all crap!
You're all rubbish
Except for cool me!'
Bewildered, the rest of the girls
Looked at each other,
Shrugged
And agreed to agree.

Because Donna was different
And no-one could beat her
At marbles

At the end of the day
Her pockets bulged heavily
And her swagger rattled across
The yard.
She made rockets and battleships
And an unholy mess in art.
Nobody called her a tomboy
(Not that she'd have cared)
Nobody dared

Because Donna was different
The way I was.
We both preferred playing with boys.
Preferred football and micromachines
To prissy, pink toys
And the simple rules of Bob-down Tig
To the boobytrapped maze
The glittering haze
Of girls' games.
The rough tough and tumble of Army
Was gentler than the sweet toxicity
Of playing Beauty Contest
With Tammy and Felicity.

But Donna was different:
Where she was a credit
To any football team
Any Lego city
I was, if I was lucky
Allowed to join in out of pity
And with Donna's sponsorship.
'Oh god, don't have her, she's right soft!'
'Don't be tight!
She can't help being posh:
She's alright!'

Because Donna was different:
She could have been a playground horror.
Her fists were like rocks
And she knew how to drop
A boy to the floor
With a shove of her knee,
But she did it with honour:
She always punched up
Fully aware of any injustice
And when her indignation was piqued
She vented the streak
That might have made her a bully
On bullies.

Donna was different.
And maybe she knew
That the only thing they didn't see
When they left her alone, and went after me
Was the sparkle, the gleam in her eye
That said 'Listen. Don't even dream
Of messing with who I was born to be.
Don't even try.'
I still think of Donna today
And how she was different,
And sometimes I borrow
Her sparkle
To wear in my eye.

## Daphne
*After the Greek myth*

I just wanted to stay free.
That was why I ran,
Ran from a God, from a boy
Who had weapons of light and throatfuls of song,
A boy who was taught that lust meant love
And love meant dominance
And dominance meant pursuit.
A boy who thought that when a girl says no
It only means you should shout a little louder,
Chase her a little further,
Though her feet may become blistered,
Though her run may become a desperate stumble,
Though her prayers may become frantic screams.

Father, you heard my screams, answered my cries.
You sent me armour
But it was made of splinters
My legs became immovable, merged themselves into a trunk.
I felt myself stiffen, my blood turning to sap,
My heartbeat suffocated by wood
My toes spreading into a network of roots,
Which chained me to the earth.
My scream silenced,
Gagged by the foul-tasting bark that grew across my mouth.
Oh, father, this was not salvation.
You turned my body into a cage,
Locking a woman inside of herself
Does not save her from what waits outside.

The boy who claimed to love me,
Who wore his divinity like a crown,

Stood and watched
As the body he desired disappeared into laurel.
Not knowing how to leave without taking something,
He used a dagger to cut gashes into my arms, hacking off a branch
Which he fashioned into a wreath,
Placed the garland of leaves in his golden hair.
He went back to Olympus,
Where he wrote poems about love and agony
And silvery tunes about a girl who became a tree.
When the wind carries his songs to me,
I weep softly, my pain like a rustle in my branches.

HOLLIE MCNISH

*Fine*

and she says 'hey, how u doing?'
and i smile 'fine' into the phone
if she'd skyped, I'd not have answered
cos then she would have known
that I am lying on my bedroom floor
a starfish on a rug
glass of wine, stinging eyes
desperate for a hug
that I worry I'm not coping
that I feel like throwing up
that I cannot keep up with my work
that I'm frightened when it's night

I ask her how *she's* doing
'oh' she says, 'I'm fine'.

## *Expectations*

you do not want to stand in front of me
to undress slowly       to unleash       each button
one
by
one
by
one
as I loll upon the bed and watch

you do not want to stand in front of me
to dance for me and stare at me—seductive
—struggling to mimic a professionally skilled stripper

you do not find it easy even just to stand
in underwear—to pose in *sexy satin pants*
to prance around the room for me
to twirl for me like catwalk turns
to be *certain* you will turn me on

you do not love it
you feel *uncomfortable, stupid*
you state—defensive—you're *un homme!*

—I know!
I just wish you would realise
(despite the posters and the films)
(despite the lingerie on buses)
(despite the billboards
and the pop porn and the
lap dance love of mtv)

we're not so different—you and me
we're not so different—you and me

LAURIE BOLGER

*Rubbish*

*And so live ever—or else swoon to death,*
that's what he said, Keats.

Although I bet he never tripped
over the recycling on his way in
*and tonight, Cilla, I'm full-on plummeting*
                    *through the concrete.*

The stars are so much brighter where you live,
they're giving everything they've got

but you are complaining about money, and that taxi
that took us all round the houses for the sake of it.

Tonight we took down every single shot and swig,
sang rubbish lyrics to sweaty ceilings
in dance floor crowds we couldn't breathe in.

Then we ditched trays of cheesy chips
like pennies lobbed into a fountain,
a sixpence buried in the Christmas pudding.

I made a wish.

*Allgemeinbildung*

—*German: meaning everything that an adult capable of living
independently can reasonably be expected to know*


That frozen sausages thrown
into a hot pan will spit
scaldingly.

That painting kitchen cupboards
brightly and with stencils
will not result in a playful
boho chic.

That it's wise to feign business as usual
for the over-eager neighbour
and not to let her in too much.

That it is difficult to ascertain
(even for the professional)
when a person has been re-abled.

That from here on the floor
the man whose kitchen
looks into mine
can't see me.

That beauty is, by and large
a simple matter of symmetry.

That wonky stencils and a shaking hand
probably won't produce symmetry.

That pain can do strange things
to the mind and body.

That it's warm and dark
in the uterus and perhaps the baby
never really wants to come out anyway.

That cats don't care if you live or die
and won't call for help in an emergency.

That unmopped lino
mulched with month-old crumbs
is surprisingly, numbingly comfy.

That if something is missing for long enough
it is almost certainly behind the fridge.

That, in the absence of answers,
nodding, saying nothing, hiding
is the holy trinity.

That the scars from scalding sausages
do not disappear overnight.

That if something is missing for long enough
it is almost certainly not behind the fridge.

KATE GARRETT

*Gravida 5, Parity 3*

The chart on the page plots her growth-climb
as I consider the five and the three above—
she is the missing number four, floating in red
limbo where her kicking heels meet the dust
of a heart-stopped lentil, left behind in my other life.

Three others held places between the two,
now echoes of fast-forward newborn mewls
fade in the voicing of views, questions,
in the quiver and swagger of young men
waiting for a tiny sister's birth.

And my little never-sprouted was the first,
a scout sent to map a universe I'll never
know—a camp these five have run to, run from,
outgrown; each marked the way for the next
with new scars, indents, like fresh cairn stones.

## Still, but not Silent

She looked long at the tongue, perfectly still
and tilted a little to one side. Lifting it, she automatically
noted the nibble marks of bruxism on either side.
She scraped a rust-dry crust from a corner of the mouth;
poked within the ears—each mysterious maze;
rifled routinely through the dark curls some lover
may have done in sensuous lingering motion;
examined the open hands—perfectly still on either side;
took careful scrapings from below the nails;
lifted each limp limb—strangely stiff and helpless.
John Doe's body lay still and primed like prize meat.

Her gaze strayed again and again to the staring eyes—
an indeterminate mud-grey that held secrets.
She rolled him over, photographed tattoos and bruises,
checked spots, swellings and abnormalities,
dictated into the hands-free recording device—
her voice a monotonous monologue invading the chamber
before her knife descended in practised moves
to slice open organs, to spread and read the entrails.
His life and death lay exposed before her—a story
of twists and turns in myriad possible directions.
John Doe lay deathly still—still, but not silent.

## Indrail Honeymoon

Indrail passes were just the ticket
for our *Bharat yatra* honeymoon.
From New Delhi we went everywhere;
checked in at railway overnight rooms.
It was monsoon time and the taxi
splashed through the flooded streets of Agra.
The Taj Mahal was entirely ours,
a blessing to seal our honeymoon.
At Pune we did the ashram rounds;
at Goa we drank wine together,
while fellow passengers' radios
blared Bollywood songs to bolster us;
a Kerala *bund* greeted our train
at Trivandrum, but our nights were sweet;
we held hands at Kanyakumari;
enjoyed the gardens of Bangalore;
and fellow travellers at Madras
wished us well and gave tips on married life:
'most of all,' they said, 'don't honeymoon;
it's a decadent Western custom.
A couple in Simla were murdered
while on honeymoon, so be careful!'
We chatted, we shared food and laughter.
Our loving relations in Vizag,
Kolkata and Jamshedpur were a joy
to embrace. We went also to Ranchi
to honour my late father-in-law
in a British military grave.
On the train ride to Varanasi,
our final exhilarating stop,
we were joined by a corpse and crowd

of relatives singing all-night hymns.
Our Indrail honeymoon train was on
a journey of marriage, life and death;
was, and still is, one great adventure.


Notes:
*Bharat yatra:* India tour
*Bund:* literally 'shut', a Kerala bund was a state-wide
industrial action when most places were shut.

AMY KINSMAN

*Untitled*

In the sparkler light,
it looks like it might be glitter on your face after all

and we could pretend
that they haven't yet drawn the sheet over his face,
over the lips beginning to blue and his still chest
that breath came to in the year
you're now letting in through the door
you will let the last of him out of.

It's a stupid old superstition
that ordinarily you would refuse to partake in

but the bells are ringing
and fireworks spinning through the air
over the houses and the roof of this hospital,
Auld Lang Syne carried on the first wind of January,
Jools Holland coming in loud and clear
despite the champagne he's singing through.

I will not remember this,
your hand tracing over my mother's swollen stomach,

my brother ready to begin
when spring starts rolling in from the south,
steadily placing one daffodil in front of the other,
learning how to falter forward on such unsteady flowers
as its hands grasp for the winter
always just a moment out of reach.

Silently you both agree
that you will not call him Bernard.

CAROL EADES

*A Curious Legacy*

Today, in the rain,
I found a dunnock egg.
Swooped down upon it,
Brought it home in teal fragility.
I thought I did this for my father.
Today I find with this egg,
I do it for myself.
As a child, scared of the dark,
You read me stories,
To ease me into sleep.
Now I read and sing to you,
To ease your anxieties.
Sleep. Don't fear the night.

SUZANNAH EVANS

*The Censored City*

Nightly the municipal workers paint
the dead grass back to its original colour.
The mouths of rush-hour pedestrians
are stopped with facemasks.

Internet searches for *painted grass*
or *municipal workers* turn up nothing.
On the grassland that belts the city
are sheep, cows, horses and camels.

The grazing ones don't look up
and those with their eyes raised
keep on staring into the distance
where the factories fill the sky with clouds.

In strong winds the herds have been known
to blow onto their backs, collect in piles
with the hollow clunking of patio furniture
until somebody comes to stand them back up.

## *How to Live in a City*

Learn to find peace in a bank queue.

Grow something for yourself
even if it's only herbs.

Go to the park to see magnolia blooms
hanging on the trees like lightbulbs.

Pool your resources; offer your spare room
to the woman who has walked from the coast
carrying on her back
everything the sea didn't swallow.

When you see a human put their hand
softly to another's face
imagine that you too
are being touched with such tenderness.

Talk to your neighbours
when you meet them in the hallway
no matter how they draw their boundaries.

Watch the news from under your duvet
record it, watch it back
repeat each word
feel the colour and shape of each syllable
rise like a firework from your throat.

NICK ALLEN's work was first published through the 'Leads to Leeds' project: http://leadstoleeds.com. Since then his poems have appeared in the *Algebra of Owls, Poetry Salzburg Review,* the *Waterworks Anthology* and the *(Un)Forced Rhubarb Anthology.* His first pamphlet, *the necessary line,* was recently published by Half Moon Books of Otley. Nick derives most of his sustenance from espressos, malt whisky, the music of Nick Cave and the writings of Cormac McCarthy.

LAMA ANDOURA is an artist, from Syria, now based in Vienna. She was born in Damascus and Studied Fine Arts at Damascus University where she specialised in Interior Design. Lama left Syria in 2013 for Lebanon; she moved from there after about two years to Austria. Lama's artworks are based on calligraphy using the Kufic font. Kufic is the oldest calligraphic form of various Arabic scripts and consists of a modified form of the old Nabataea script. Kufic developed around the end of the 7th century in Kufa, Iraq, from which it takes its name. @Andouralama.

CHARLOTTE ANSELL has three poetry collections published by Flipped Eye with a third forthcoming in April 2017. Publications include *Poetry Review, Mslexia, Now Then* and *Butcher's Dog* and anthologies including *The Very Best of 52* and *WordLife.* She was the winner of the Red Shed Open Poetry Competition and one of 6 finalists in the Fun Palaces Write Science competition in 2015 and winner of the Watermarks Poetry Competition 2016.

CATHERINE AYRES is a teacher who lives and works in Northumberland. In 2015, she came third in the Hippocrates Prize and in 2016 she won the Elbow Room Poetry Prize. Her collection, *Amazon,* is published by Indigo Dreams.

LIZ BERRY's debut collection *Black Country* (Chatto & Windus, 2014), described as 'a sooty, soaring hymn to her native West

Midlands' (*Guardian*), was a PBS Recommendation, received a Somerset Maugham Award, won the Geoffrey Faber Memorial Award and the Forward Prize for Best First Collection 2014.

JACOB BLAKESLEY is a Leverhulme Early Career Fellow in Translation Studies at the University of Leeds. He has published a monograph on modern Italian poet-translators: *Modern Italian Poets: Translators of the Impossible* (University of Toronto, 2014). He has published poetry translations in *Chicago Quarterly Review, Chicago Review, Comparative Critical Studies, Journal of Italian Translation, Poetry Miscellany,* and *Stand.* He is the translator of *Great Italian Short Stories of the Twentieth-Century* (Dover Books, 2013).

London Laureate LAURIE BOLGER was born in London W10. Laurie currently hosts BANG Said the Gun, London's leading stand-up poetry night and multi award winning poetry podcast Round @ Laurie's. Laurie is lead facilitator for BBC 1Xtra's *Words First* and her poetry has appeared on BBC World Service and Radio 1. Her debut poetry collection *Box Rooms* was released by Burning Eye Books earlier this year. www.lauriebolger.com

MALIKA BOOKER is a British poet and multi-disciplinary artist of Guyanese and Grenadian Parentage. *Breadfruit,* a pamphlet (flippedeye, 2007), was recommended by the Poetry Society and her poetry collection *Pepper Seed* (Peepal Tree Press, 2013) was longlisted for the OCM Bocas prize and shortlisted for the Seamus Heaney Centre prize for first full collection (2014). She is published with the poets Sharon Olds and Warsan Shire in *The Penguin Modern Poet Series 3: Your Family: Your Body* (2017). Malika has been the recipient of residencies from Millay Colony, Cove Park, The India International Centre and Kocevje through The Centre for Slovenian Literature. She is a Fellow of both The Complete Works and Cave Canem and was inaugural Poet in Residence at the Royal Shakespeare Company. Malika has an MA in Creative and Life Writing from Goldsmiths University and is currently the Douglas Caster Cultural Fellow in Creative Writing at University of Leeds.

S J BRADLEY is a writer from Leeds, UK. Her short fiction has been published in the US and UK, including in *Litro Magazine, Queen Mob's,* and *New Willesden Short Stories 7.* She is the organiser behind non-profit literary social Fictions of Every Kind, and director of the Northern Short Story Festival. Her second novel, *Guest,* is out now on Dead Ink Books www.deadinkbooks.com

CAROLE BROMLEY lives in York where she is the stanza rep and runs poetry surgeries for The Poetry Society. Twice a winner in the Poetry Business Book and Pamphlet Competition, she has two pamphlets and two books with Smith/Doorstop, the most recent being *The Stonegate Devil* (2015). Her first collection of poems for children, *Blast Off!* will be published in 2017. www.carolebromleypoetry.co.uk

Indian-born writer and arts psychotherapist DEBJANI CHATTERJEE, MBE, has had over 65 books of poetry and prose published for children and adults. She is a Royal Literary Writing Fellow and Survivors' Poetry Patron. The critic Barry Tebb describes her as a 'national treasure'. Poetry prizes include a Peterloo Poets Prize, Muse India's Poetry in Translation First Prize and Word Masala's Lifetime Achievement in Poetry Award. Her latest poetry collection is *Do You Hear the Storm Sing?*

After graduating from York University in English Literature and teaching English in secondary schools for years, LOUISE CLINES finally decided to start writing herself. She is married to Jeremy and is mother to Esther (7) and Nathaniel (5). Her poetry is often about family life and motherhood as well as being influenced by her passion for social justice, environmental issues and Green political beliefs. She is based in Sheffield and is a member of the Broomspring Writers.

HANNAH COPLEY writes poetry and teaches literature and creative writing in universities and schools. Her poems have been published in a number of magazines and anthologies, including *Stand, Poetry and Audience, Templar's Skein,* and *Agenda*. She was highly commended in the 2015 Faber New Poets Prize, the 2017 International Hippocrates Prize, and the 2017 YorkMix competition. She is currently working on her first collection.

BETH DAVIES writes poetry and short fiction and is a member of Hive South Yorkshire Young Writers group. In 2014, she won the overall first prize in Writing Yorkshire's Photofictions competition. Her work is forthcoming or has been published by Writing Yorkshire (*Everyday Hymn* anthology), Paper Swans, Young Poets Network and the *Hive South Yorkshire anthology 2017*. She is currently on a gap year before going to Durham University next year to study philosophy.

CAROL EADES is an aspergic polymath DIY enthusiast. They are the holder of multiple degrees in various subjects, and they live in Sheffield with multiple pets of various species. Carol has published work in various webzines and anthologies and has performed across South Yorkshire.

SUZANNAH EVANS lives in Sheffield. Her pamphlet *Confusion Species* was published as a winner of the 2012 Poetry Business competition and in 2013 she received a Northern Writers' Award. She has published her work in magazines including *The London Magazine, The Rialto, Magma, The North* and *Poetry Review*.

BASHAR FARAHAT is a doctor, from Syria, now working at a school in London and planning to re-qualify to practise medicine in the UK. He was born in a small village in northern Syria and studied medicine at Aleppo University. At the start of the uprising against the Al Assad regime, Bashar was training to become a paediatrician. Twice Bashar was detained by the government regime, accused of participation in demonstrations, writing to support peaceful activities and helping wounded demonstrators in a field hospital. When he was released a second time, faced with the prospect of having to do military service or a third period of detention, Bashar escaped to Lebanon. He was subsequently selected, in 2015, to move to the UK and given humanitarian protection, being settled initially in Bradford. Bashar has always written poetry. He gave readings whilst studying medicine and, since arriving in the UK, has given readings in Arabic and in his own English translations.

KATE GARRETT is the founding editor of Three Drops Press and the web journal *Picaroon Poetry*. Her own work has been widely published online and in print, and her pamphlet *The Density of Salt* (Indigo Dreams, 2016) was longlisted for a Saboteur Award in 2016. Her pamphlet *You've never seen a doomsday like it* was published by Indigo Dreams in 2017. She lives in Sheffield.

KATHERINE HENDERSON is a poet/blogger/essayist based in Edinburgh and a graduate of the Writing Squad. Her blog *Pin Ups and Panic Attacks* explores vintage fashion, mental health and self-care. She dabbles in crafting and embroidery. She is working on a series of drawings called #projectladybutts that celebrates all kinds of femme beauty.

JO IRWIN is currently completing a novel for children as part of her MA Writing course at Sheffield Hallam University. She spent some time travelling and searching for stories before settling on the edge of the Peak District, where she endeavours to put the ideas she accumulated into words. Jo also writes poetry and short stories and teaches English in Secondary Schools.

AMY KINSMAN is a genderfluid poet and playwright from Manchester, England. As well as being the founding editor of Riggwelter Press and associate editor of *Three Drops From A Cauldron*, they are also the host of Gorilla Poetry, a regular open mic in Sheffield. Their work has appeared, or is forthcoming, in many publications, including *Amaryllis, Clear Poetry, Picaroon Poetry, Prole* and *Rat's Ass Review.*

ETHEL MAQEDA lives in Sheffield where she's finishing a PhD in Literature & Creative Writing. Her writing is inspired by the storytelling traditions of her native Zimbabwe. She has had short stories published in *English PEN Magazine, Big Writing for a Small World* and in the University of Sheffield's creative writing journal, *Route 57.* When she's not writing or watching theatre, Ethel spends time in Cape Town trying to micro-parent her two teenage sons.

CHAR MARCH grew up in Scotland (of Yorkshire parents) and worked extensively with the deaf community, and within dance. She's won many awards for poetry, short fiction and as a playwright. Her credits include: five poetry collections including *The Thousand Natural Shocks*, a short story collection *Something Vital Fell Through*, six BBC Radio 4 plays, and seven stage plays. She is a Hawthornden Fellow, and has been Writer-in-Residence to the NHS, international business schools, art galleries, and huge landscape projects.

HOLLIE MCNISH loves writing poetry. She has published three collections, *Papers, Cherry Pie,* and *Plum,* and one poetic memoir *Nobody Told Me,* of which the *Scotsman* suggested 'The world needs this book'. In 2016 she co-wrote a play *Offside* relating the two hundred year history of UK women's football, as well as collaborating on her second poetry album *Versus* with the brilliant Dutch Metropole Orkest. Hollie tours continuously across the UK and is a big fan of online readings—her poetry videos have attracted millions of views worldwide. She has a keen interest in migration, infant health and language learning and does readings for organisations as diverse as The Economist, MTV, and UNICEF. *Plum*, her first poetry collection with Picador, relating her thoughts on fruit, flesh and society, was published in summer 2017.

MIMI MESFIN (YENENESH) has been in the UK since July 2015. She is a poet and writes in Amharic and has performed her poetry across South Yorkshire. Mimi qualified as a nurse in Ethiopia and is currently busy learning English and she hopes to find care work looking after the elderly.

VICKY MORRIS writes poetry and short stories, and supports young people to write and find their voice. She has been published by places like *Butcher's Dog, The Interpreter's House, Matter,* Silver Birch Press, and *Ink, Sweat & Tears.* In 2013 she made the documentary *Dyslexic and Loving Words* (YouTube). Vicky won a Northern Writers Award in 2014 for fiction, and was shortlisted for the Jerwood/Arvon Mentoring Scheme for poetry 2016/17. Her website is www.vickymorris.co.uk.

SAI MURRAY's debut poetry collection, *Ad-liberation,* was published in 2013. Clean from advertising for over 17 years, Sai now runs artist/activist promotions agency Liquorice Fish. He is a founding poet facilitator of the youth arts campaigning program Voices that Shake!; resident poet at Numbi; and was lead writer on Virtual Migrants 2015 touring production, *Continent Chop Chop.* His poetry and short stories feature in the anthologies: *Red; Closure; Creative Freedom; Tangled Roots* and *Dance The Guns to Silence.*

WENDY PRATT was born in Scarborough in 1978. Her work has been widely published in journals and magazines and has featured in several anthologies, including *The Forward Anthology* and *The Emergency Poet.* Her first pamphlet, *Nan Hardwicke Turns into a Hare* was published by Prolebooks, they also published her first full collection, *Museum Pieces.* Her latest pamphlet, *Lapstrake,* is published by Flarestack Poets, and her latest collection, *Gifts the Mole Gave Me,* was published by Valley Press in October 2017.

SHELLEY ROCHE-JACQUES' poetry has appeared in magazines such as *Magma, The Rialto* and *The Boston Review*. Her pamphlet *Ripening Dark* is part of the Eyewear 20/20 series, and her debut full collection is due out with Eyewear in 2017. She teaches Creative Writing at Sheffield Hallam University, and is particularly interested in the dramatic monologue as a way of examining social and political issues.

SHIRIN TEIFOURI's research has explored pedagogical engagement with the function of literature, specifically poetry, linked to cross-cultural narratives of exile, displacement, 'statelessness', and mental health. She has designed and developed a range of projects in collaboration with 'socially marginalized individuals' from different ethnic backgrounds, charities, community partners, libraries and art groups.

SEZ THOMASIN is an autistic, genderqueer poet living in Sheffield. They have written limericks about sex and gender for Kate Bornstein's *My New Gender Workbook* and have won several poetry slams including Poetstars 2008, Wordlife 2010 & 2016, and the Sheffield Antislam. They were a semi-finalist at the 2017 Hammer and Tongue slam. One of these days they'll do a book.

RIVER WOLTON is a former Derbyshire Poet Laureate whose collections include *Leap* and *Indoor Skydiving* (published by Smith/Doorstop). She recently edited *Courage of Conscience: Imagined Voices of the First World War*, collaborating with young people to research and write about conscientious objectors. She has worked extensively with community writing and arts projects, particularly with marginalised groups such as refugees and asylum-seekers.

WARDA YASSIN is a GCSE English teacher at a Sheffield school and a recreational poet at night. She has performed alongside the likes of Buddy Wakefield, Jean Binta Breeze and Hollie Mc-Nish and loves the works and words of Warsan Shire, Hannah

Lowe, Kim Moore and Chimamanda Ngozi Adichie. She is a graduate of the Writing Squad and writes about her family, culture, and the spaces and gaps in between these two worlds. Her main source of inspirations are her grandmothers and their vivid and infinite tales.

*

## About the Editors

HELEN MORT is a poet and fiction writer born in Sheffield. She is the author of two poetry collections, *Division Street* (2013) and *No Map Could Show Them* (2016), both published by Chatto & Windus. She's also the editor of *Lake District Trail Running* (Vertebrate) and *The Owl and the Pussycat*, an anthology of poems for children. Her first novel is forthcoming from Chatto & Windus. Helen is a lecturer in the Manchester Writing School at Manchester Metropolitan University and occasionally writes for Radio 3 and Radio 4.

RACHEL BOWER is a poet and Leverhulme Research Fellow at the University of Leeds. Rachel's pamphlet, *Moon Milk*, will be published by Valley Press in April 2018. Her book, *Epistolarity and World Literature*, 1980–2010, was published by Palgrave Macmillan in October 2017. Rachel is currently working on a second academic monograph which investigates the links between poets in Leeds and Nigeria in the 1950s and 60s. Rachel reviews regularly for various magazines and journals, including *Stand* and *Wasafiri*, and is the founder of *Verse Matters*, a feminist arts collective in Sheffield.